Your Purpose Has Not Plateaued

Kaitlin Miller

Copyright © 2023 Kaitlin Miller

All rights reserved. No part of this publication may be reproduced, distributed, or transmitted in any form or by any means, including photocopying, recording, or other electronic or mechanical methods, without the prior written permission of the publisher, except in the case of brief quotations embodied in critical reviews and certain other noncommercial uses permitted by copyright law. For permission requests, write to the publisher, addressed "Attention: Permissions Coordinator," at the address below.

ISBN: 979-8-218-26071-2 (Paperback)

First printing edition 2023

120 Publishing House

PO Box 1010,

Thonotosassa, FL.

www.120dayspublishing.com

DEDICATION

I dedicate this book to my incredible family: my loving husband, Eric Miller, and two amazing children. Their unwavering support, boundless love, and infinite patience have been the pillars that sustained me throughout this journey. Without them, this accomplishment would not have been possible.

I also extend my dedication to my dear friend and mentor, Taushauna Burrel. It is her encouragement and guidance that propelled me to embark on this writing adventure and see it through to completion. She has been there for me every step of the way, playing a pivotal role in my personal transformation as well.

Finally, I extend my dedication to my incredible, supportive parents. To my mother, whose unwavering availability and willingness to lend an ear allowed me to bounce ideas and thoughts around, I am immensely grateful. It is from her that I inherited my love for writing. To my father, who has always told me I could do anything I wanted. His unwavering support and encouragement have given me the confidence to pursue my dreams.

Your Purpose Has Not Plateaued

CONTENTS

Chapter 1	The Magic Words	10
Chapter 2	Hope Again	21
Chapter 3	Surroundings and Seasons	38
Chapter 4	Change the Narrative	55
Chapter 5	Transformation	63
Chapter 6	The importance of our mind	73
Chapter 7	The Victory	81

ACKNOWLEDGMENTS

I would like to acknowledge my extraordinary family, parents, and cherished mentor. This book is a testament to the profound impact you have had on my life and my creative endeavors. You have been my constant source of inspiration and strength. Thank you for believing in me and being a significant part of my journey. I love you all!

I would also like to acknowledge my Pastor, Robert Tisdale, and express my gratitude for his profound influence on my spiritual and mental transformation. His teachings have played a significant role in shaping my journey, and I am forever grateful.

PREFACE

In the depths of despair and the grip of hopelessness, a flickering ember of light ignited within me. It was a revelation that has forever changed my life and, hopefully, the lives of countless others. It is this revelation, this unwavering truth, that forms the foundation of "Your Purpose Has Not Plateaued."

This book is not a mere collection of words; it is a beacon of hope, a guiding hand, and a testament to the power of perseverance and faith. It is an invitation to all those who find themselves sinking in despair, feeling trapped and purposeless, to rise above their circumstances and embrace the truth that they are not stuck where they are.

Through the pages of this book, I will share my personal testimony and take you on a transformative journey. It is a journey that requires soul searching, the courage to let go of what no longer serves us, and the determination to embrace the elements necessary for success.

In the midst of my darkest hours, I found solace in the words spoken to me by God. The wisdom, guidance, and unwavering love of God illuminated my path, and it is with gratitude that I share these words with you. May they touch your heart, inspire your spirit, and empower you to seek after hope and your purpose with unwavering faith.

With each turn of the page, I invite you to open your heart and mind. Allow the inspired message of this book to awaken the dormant dreams within you, to rekindle the flame of hope, and to reignite your belief in the potential that resides within you.

With love,
Kaitlin Miller

Your Purpose Has Not Plateaued

CHAPTER 1

THE MAGIC WORDS

One day I found myself in a foreign place. There I was, lying face down on my hardwood floors, desperately crying out to God to save me from this hopeless state of mind I had been trapped in. Honestly, I felt as if I were drowning in despair and hopelessness. While I didn't know how to get myself out, I knew I was so tired of feeling this way. I was desperate to be relieved and restored from the state of hopelessness that trapped me. Have you ever been there? Have you been somewhere you didn't want to be mentally and/or spiritually, but you didn't know how to bring yourself out of it or just didn't have the strength to do it? Have you been in a place where you just knew there was more to life than what was currently before you? You just knew there had to be more than the stress, more than the ever-revolving, never changing day-to-day life you're living. Maybe you asked, "There has to be peace and success in the future somewhere for me, right?" Have you experienced this but had no idea how to obtain the "more" from life? Maybe even to the point where it overwhelmed you, and you just gave up, stopped dreaming, and counted it as lost? Have you ever been so disappointed in yourself for where you were in life? Have you ever let that disappointment in yourself cause you to throw in the towel and give up, or at least want to? You know you should be doing more or better than you currently are, but you just don't know how to bring yourself out of this funk or out of this feeling of hopelessness to achieve anything. Well, I have been there, and I questioned, "How could this be me?" I looked over my life and knew how blessed I was. I had beautiful kids, a great, hard-working husband, a beautiful house, and family that loved and supported me. I became so convicted for allowing myself to even get to this point. How did I get to this point, you may ask? Let me share my story with you.

 I was a stay-at-home mom of two young boys whom I loved immensely, only two years apart. They were my everyday life; from the time I woke up to the time I went to sleep, there was no separation from them. Everything I did was for them; it was like I had totally lost myself in them. At the time, I wasn't complaining because they were the greatest gifts I could have ever received. However, I started to realize I didn't recognize myself. How could I, though? I totally neglected myself to be the best mother I could be for them, giving them literally all of me until I no longer recognized myself. To be honest, the way that I viewed being a mother was giving your absolute ALL to your children: all of your attention, all of your time, and all of your focus. But in reality, what I ended up learning is that in doing so, not only do you neglect yourself in many areas, but you also can't give your best to your children when you're pouring from an empty cup. Here's something to think about: if you are depleted mentally, emotionally, or even physically, then what are you really giving your children? As you ponder that, let me continue with the story. Through the continual exhaustion and the extensive mothering nature that I took on, I lost myself. I gave my all to my children and forgot about me. I put myself on the back burner and convinced myself that my children needed me more than I needed anything. At this particular time, I was also dealing with crippling anxiety. The anxiety itself isolated me even more because I felt I couldn't handle going out anywhere, so I just stayed home all the time in my safe place. It even affected my spiritual life. My prayer life was suffering. I couldn't tell you how long it had been since I picked up the bible to read it. I convinced myself there was just not enough time in the day. I convinced myself that since my children constantly surrounded me, there was no time that I could get away and pray. Let alone enough quiet time to read and study the bible. Little did I know that neglecting my spiritual life would be synonymous with rendering myself defenseless to hopelessness. On top of all these things, I was also dealing with trauma from previous traumatic experiences, from severe sickness to birth complications, and I never really dealt with it or released it; I just learned to live with it. All of these things together would be what caused me to no longer recognize myself and begin the downhill journey toward hopelessness. Years later, as my children grew older, I found myself still in the same place. I still felt like I was stuck, not going anywhere, with no forward movement, no purpose, and no direction. Just still only being a mother and going through the daily grind of the same mundane tasks as the days before. I simply didn't know how to get myself out of this hole I put myself in, so I just stayed there. Upon talking to many other mothers, I realized quickly that this is a common theme. Mothers will lose themselves in their maternal duties and fail to care for themselves in a way that is greatly needed. In all honesty, it can become incredibly hard to juggle all that life throws at us, especially within our day-to-day tasks, to the point that we then pick the "most important" things (which are often influenced by society or social media) to focus on to not become too overwhelmed. Guess what ONE of those "most important" things we picked is not? Yep, you guessed it, ourselves. Nine times out of ten, we mothers do NOT pick ourselves. We often do not put ourselves as a priority. For a simple example, we might say, "Oh, this laundry is everywhere! If anyone sees this, they will think I'm a slob. I guess I need to fold it and put it away." When in reality, you may not have been able to shower in a couple of days, and a nice hot shower with some quiet time will probably make you feel way better than putting that laundry away. So, instead of choosing something that would benefit your mental state, you choose something that society deems as more important. It isn't until we are drowning in hopelessness and unrecognition of self-identity that we are even made aware of this problem. I was "that" mother. That mother who loved her family so fiercely but still felt lost and hopeless and thought that the only thing I would ever amount to be was a mother. I mean, how could I even begin to have time for anything else when I am swamped with laundry, constantly picking up after two toddlers, feeding them, then making time to sit and play with them, and all the many other things stay-at-home moms do? While some mothers may be completely content with only ever being a mother, I was not ok with that because I felt God had given me many other talents/gifts and even callings that I wanted to use for his glory and be successful in. I began to remember those dreams and ambitions I once had for my life and the callings I felt over my life before becoming a mother and realized how far away and impossible they now seemed. I eagerly and desperately wanted to know success outside of motherhood but had no vision of what that would look like or how that could ever happen. For me, that is when hopelessness set in. The moment I realized those previous dreams felt so far away that I could barely remember them, the moment I felt stuck and didn't know how to break free, the moment I thought I would never move from the position I was in, the moment I felt my purpose in life had plateaued. Friends, once hopelessness sets in, it's just a slippery slope down to regret and then depression. Once this mudslide happens, it seems almost impossible to see a way out. So much so you begin to stop looking for a way out and start to believe this is where you'll be forever. You begin to believe you're stuck and this is all life has for you. You stop dreaming. As a matter of fact, you don't even know how to dream anymore? You question, "What even is a dream?" You may feel like you have these gifts and talents but no opportunities or direction, all these bottled-up ambitions with no way to release them. I was this person. I simply could no longer see/envision a future of my success. My Pastor, Robert Tisdale, recently made this statement, "If you can't remember who you are, then you can't really know where you're going." And oh, how this story proves this statement true! My state of hopelessness caused me to not recognize who I was. It blinded me, crippled me, and also deafened me to the word and promises of God concerning my life. I allowed my state of hopelessness to draw me away from the true purpose and plan God had already ordained for my life from the beginning. I had forgotten who I was in God and also seemed to forget who he was. I allowed all these circumstances to seem bigger in my eyes than the God of the universe, the God that I serve and gave my life to. In this moment of realization, I found myself crying out to God like never before for help. I told him where I was. I began to tell him how I felt. I believe I cried out because I just knew there was more for me, and I had a burning desire to attain it, but I couldn't see a way out of the hopelessness I felt. I didn't know how to get to the "more" for my life. For me, my desperate cry was like a "hail mary." I knew if God did not step in, I would be swept away in this awful mudslide! As I laid face down on my floor, I cried out and told God I no longer wanted to be in this state of mind, and I wanted to be delivered and set free. In this moment, God spoke so clearly to me; it was honestly the first time I'd ever heard something so clearly. He said these five powerful words, "YOUR PURPOSE HAS NOT PLATEAUED." I cried out and kept hearing these words. I paused for a moment, and then I realized these words were the answer to my prayer! I was curious about the word "plateaued," so I looked it up in the dictionary to understand its meaning. According to the online dictionary, it means "to reach a state or level of little or no growth or decline, especially to stop increasing or progressing." My tears then started to change from sorrow to joy! I knew this was God promising me there was MORE to my story. The best was NOT behind me but in front of me! I got up and started rejoicing and claiming that promise. My purpose has not plateaued! There IS more for me! A promise that I am not stuck where I am and that there is always a way out when God is involved! These five words are what I consider "the magic words" because they catapulted me into my transformation. While rejoicing over this word God had given me, I felt him impart to me that this word was not just for me but for many others who may be in the same situation and mindset. My purpose with this book is to encourage you and to help you get out of the drowning mudslide of hopelessness and to step into the promises of God and the purpose he has for your life!

I want to start by expounding a little more on what I mentioned briefly above about knowing who you are.

Recently my Pastor preached on the importance of knowing who you are and knowing who God is. Who would have known that it would speak to me so profoundly years later, as I was once in this place? I had already written a good portion of this book, and when he preached it, I immediately knew I had to share it in this book. He shared the concept of two confessions: 1. The realization of who God is. That he is sovereign and totally in control of every facet of our human experience. 2. The awareness of who you are in God and that there is a purpose God has specifically prepared for you. He mentioned merging these two confessions so that you can become all that God has envisioned for you to become. So, to clarify, by aligning what we perceive and what we believe, we open ourselves to the transformative journey of coming into our God-given purpose. You may be asking, how is that? Understand that merging these two concepts allows us to see ourselves through God's eyes, viewing ourselves as a vessel of divine purpose. This perspective shift can lead you to step out of your comfort zone, pursue your passions, and serve others with love and compassion. Yes, grasping this simple concept and applying it to your daily life can really make this kind of difference! I can definitely look back and say I lacked this concept of realization and therefore found myself lost and hopeless. Through my experiences, I can testify that this concept is most definitely needed for you to live a good, hopeful, and overcoming life. If I did not finally surrender my negativity and hopelessness to God in prayer, who knows where I would be today? If I did not finally recognize that he was the only one who could pull me from this place I was bound in and that he is sovereign enough to hold my world in his hands, where would I be today? If I did not choose to believe that there had to be more for me than where I was and what I was going through, again, I ask, where would I be today? I wholeheartedly believe I would not be here writing this book under the anointing of the Holy Spirit, sending a message to others who may be suffering or have suffered the same as I that there is most definitely MORE waiting for you! I believe that this concept, along with others we will talk about in this book, combined with your actions, will bring you to the deliverance and the purpose that was designed only for you! Will you believe with me? My friends, believing is seriously half the battle. And it's one of the simplest things you can do. We all believe in something. It's just a matter of deciding what you're going to believe in. You may say, "It's hard for me to believe." But if you look at your day-to-day life, our days are filled with belief. How, you may ask? Do you believe that when you turn on the stove to cook your food, it will come on? Do you think twice about what will happen when you turn the knob? Probably not! Without second thought or hesitation, you just know and believe that the stove is going to come on. I could add more examples, but I'm sure you get the picture. Belief is defined as "An acceptance that a statement is true or that something exists" and "trust, faith, or confidence in someone or something." So, let's start by accepting "your purpose has not plateaued" as a true statement for your life and having confidence in yourself to pursue and reach your purpose!

Reflective Questions

Ask yourself these questions and grab a journal/notebook to write down your answers.

1. Have you ever reached a point in your life where you felt lost and hopeless? How did you navigate through that state of hopelessness? If you have not done so yet, how can you start?

2. Have you ever neglected your own spiritual and emotional well-being while focusing solely on your responsibilities and obligations to others? How did this impact your sense of fulfillment and connection to your own purpose?

3. Have you ever felt like there was more you wanted to do or should do in this life but didn't know how to attain it? What are some things you can do to get you on the right track to attain more from life?

PRAYER

Dear Heavenly Father,
Lord, I thank you for always hearing my cry and for speaking words of life and encouragement into my heart. Grant me the desire to seek You, to read Your word, and to nurture my relationship with You. Grant me the strength to confront and release my burdens, allowing your healing touch to restore my spirit. Remind me that in You, I find peace, strength, and direction. I pray You would open my eyes to the possibilities and opportunities that lie ahead and guide me towards the path You have prepared for me. Lord, instill in me a belief in myself and in Your promises. Help me merge the realization of who you are with the awareness of who I am in you. Help me realize that my past does not define my future and that through faith and trust in You, I can overcome any obstacle. Help me understand that taking care of myself is not selfish but a necessary step towards fulfilling the purpose you have for me. I ask for the courage to step out of the place of hopelessness and into the abundant life you have prepared for me. Fill me with hope, vision, and a renewed sense of purpose. Grant me the wisdom and discernment to make choices that align with your will for my life. Help me to believe that my purpose has not plateaued and that there is always more to my story.
In Jesus Name, Amen.

CHAPTER 2

HOPE AGAIN

Have you ever wondered what hope really means? According to the dictionary, it's "a feeling of expectation and desire for a certain thing to happen." However, I love T.D. Jakes's definition of hope. He describes it as "a confident expectation that good things are coming our way." In this chapter, we will explore the essence of hope—its nature, significance, and the profound role it plays in shaping our beliefs, choices, and outlook on life. However, before we dive in further on hope, I would like to first expound on the concept of being hopeless and why we should try to avoid it at all costs. It is said that hopelessness can seriously negatively affect mental, emotional, and physical health and can interfere with an individual's ability to lead a fulfilling and meaningful life. We can also find that hopelessness can contribute to developing or exacerbating mental health disorders such as depression and anxiety. Without hope, we are directionless, and our efforts can become aimless and unproductive. How can you enter a state of hopelessness, you may ask? Great question. Through research, we can find that there are many different ways you can slip into hopelessness. It can happen due to the symptoms of post-traumatic stress disorder (PTSD) or stressful or difficult life events. It can occur from feeling incredibly overwhelmed or stagnant in life or even from dealing with a mental disorder. Surprisingly, it can also be from experiencing rejection. The point is that hopelessness can come from many different angles and cause serious negative effects. It is important that you are aware of the seriousness of hopelessness. With that being said, let's now shift our focus to the topic of hope. Why is Hope so important? Hope gives us something to aim for. When we have hope, we have a vision of a better future that we can work towards. This vision inspires us to take action and make positive changes in our lives. It gives us the motivation we need to keep pushing forward, even when things get tough. Hope can also provide a sense of purpose. When we have hope, we have a reason to get up in the morning and face the day ahead. We have a sense of meaning and direction in our lives, which can help us to find joy and fulfillment in even the most mundane tasks. Without hope, we are lost, we become stuck, and we can easily become trapped in a cycle of negativity and despair. I'm sure many of us have experienced moments in our lives where we may have lost hope. It could have been due to a health diagnosis, a job loss, or a failed relationship maybe. The point is that there are many challenges life throws at us and moments that we face that make us want to throw in the towel and give up. It's in these hard, challenging, and discouraging times that we may feel as if we are drowning in a sea of uncertainty. But understand, my friends; it's in these very moments that hope can become your lifeline. Do you hear me? Hope can keep you afloat when your current life circumstances seem to be drowning you. Picture with me for a moment, raging waters all around you and overtaking you as you struggle to keep your head above water. Now, picture someone throwing you a life jacket. You quickly put it on, and now you are floating above the water that tried to pull you under. Hope is that life jacket. When you feel the raging waters of life overtaking you, go ahead and put on hope as your life jacket so that you can float above those circumstances and not drown in hopelessness! Let hope be your confidence to keep moving forward and to stay afloat despite what you see in front of you or around you. That, my friends, is what hope can do!

I understand the significance of hope from my own personal experiences. I've faced numerous challenges over the years, from health scares to financial struggles, loss, and many other things. In the first chapter, I shared a story about a time in my life when I laid my hope down and began to drown. However, I want to share with you a time in my life when I used hope as a life jacket. I began a journey to transform my mind and was healing and being strengthened in my faith and hope from my previously mentioned state of hopelessness. During this time, I experienced moments that had me feeling like I was on a mountaintop. I mean, I was so stoked about life and my future. My faith was soaring! Big things were happening, life-changing things. Everything was going so smoothly and perfectly. Doors were continuously opening for me and my family from left and right. We received financial blessings we couldn't believe. It was easily one of the greatest moments of my life. I felt faith, hope, happiness, and purpose like I've never felt before! My season truly changed for the better. Everyone around me was getting blessed too. It was the perfect calm after a horrible storm, and I was on cloud nine. Just as my newfound hope was soaring, here came some crazy wind and rain that showered down on our lives. Everything suddenly wasn't going perfectly right anymore. Open doors were now closing. Financial blessings ceased. Those big things happening began to fall apart. I tried so hard not to take it personally and not to lose hope and give up. I had just made a major transformation in my mind, and my hope, and it took a lot of hard work; I did not want to see it slip away and be all for nothing. So, I strapped on the life jacket of hope and floated above the raging waters of life's circumstances. To keep hold of my hope, I watched what I allowed to come out of my mouth. I put to the test all the training and information I had received about transforming your mind to positivity, and I tried to stay as positive as I possibly could. I made sure I didn't let up on my prayer life and reading the Word of God, even though inside, I was confused and upset. The way everything just suddenly collapsed in our life would have had you expecting us to give up and drown in the raging waters of hopelessness. But when I say I fought it off as hard as I could, I fought y'all. I refused to let go of my hope. Even though everything around me seemed to be falling apart, I made up my mind that I would not fall apart. I was not going back to hopelessness. I leaned on God and the encouraging, uplifting people in my life a lot in this moment. I'm going to take a quick sidebar here and insert a little life lesson. You do not need people speaking into your life who will agree with everything you say, sulk in your woes with you, and validate your negative mindset. If you're calling friends or family to vent and they are not speaking up against your feelings of hopelessness, calling out or challenging your negativity, and encouraging you to course correct, then friend, you're not talking to the right people. You need people who will encourage you to stand firm, fight, be hopeful, stay positive, and be courageous. You need to be talking to those who will have the tough but constructive conversations. Returning to the story, I received a lot of encouragement and had some honest conversations with God. As a result, I was able to cling to hope as if it was my lifeline. I spoke to my circumstances before me and told them about my God. I reminded myself that the same God who allowed everything to come together for our good previously is the same yesterday, today, and forever and he changes not! I looked at the trials as a lesson being learned and found things in my life worthy of praise to focus on. I held on to my hope, my "confident expectation that good things were coming my way." I didn't look at this trial or circumstance as the end of it all; I viewed it as just a bump in the road because, ahead, I just knew better was coming. Was it easy? Not at all. Did it take determination and consistency? Yes, it did, lots of it. But if you can get into the word of God, develop a personal relationship with him, and believe his promises are for you, it makes it much easier to hope!

Although I have not yet included scripture in this text, I plan to incorporate passages from the Bible throughout because I truly and firmly believe that the word of God is a lamp unto our feet and a light unto our path (Psalms 119:105) and is needed to effectively take this journey toward hope and positivity to find our purpose. As I reflect on the verse above, I remember being in prayer one day, and God had placed this verse on my mind as I was praying. As it came to my mind, I immediately had a vision concerning this scripture. I remember seeing woods surrounding me with all kinds of trees hovering over me. I saw bushes and tree limbs that had fallen to the ground and an overgrowth of weeds coming up from the dirt. I then saw the back of a man walking in front of me. As I stood still and watched him, he started walking down what seemed to be a path, but the path could barely be seen due to all the fallen branches, overgrown bushes, and vines covering the ground. He began to pick up tree limbs and branches that were on the path and throw them to the side. He pulled up vines and overgrowth of bushes and weeds that could cause him to trip or not be able to see the path. He swept to the side with his foot, fallen leaves on the ground. It then dawned on me what he was doing. He was going before me to make sure the path was SEEN. To ensure that I could see the path and that there were no obstacles that could hinder me from knowing where I was supposed to go and getting to where I was supposed to be. My God! I began to think about the above scripture and asked myself, "What does light do for us?" It makes things seen, right? When you go into a dark room to find something, you turn the light on so that thing you're looking for can be seen. That word kept ringing in my mind and heart, "SEEN!" And I felt God saying, "You're not going to wonder which way to go or where to place your next step because I'm the lamp that guides your steps and the light that makes your path seen!" What a revelation it is! He is the light that makes our path seen! I don't believe it was ever God's will for us to wander around in this life and not know or see the path or purpose he has for us. I can say that because, through David's experience with God, he could proclaim that the word of God had been a lamp unto his feet and a light unto his path. And by this experience, we should be able to apply it to our lives because God changes not. He's the same God right now as back then. This verse is inspiration and direction for us to lean on God and the promises of his word, apply them to our lives, and watch God make our path clear and seen. What a mighty God that would walk a beaten, messy, dangerous path before me so I didn't have to! My friend, if you are walking a path where you feel lost and confused, that is not the will of God. You may be trying to find a path on your own instead of letting God lead you to the path he has already made "seen" for you. I would implore you to seek him, get into his word, and let it be the light to your path. A path straight to him and straight to your purpose. In conclusion to this vision, I began walking down the cleared pathway, and out of nowhere, it started to rain hard. Now, I believe this rain was symbolic of the trials and storms of life because as the rain came down and I continued walking, I began to have to squint my eyes as the water was falling into my eyes. My eyes became blurry from the water, and consequently, I began to lose sight of the path. I can definitely connect this to the rain or trials of life. For instance, suddenly, your washer and dryer decide to quit working, then a couple of days later, your refrigerator goes out, and a few days later, your spouse loses their job. These things in life can get you so bogged down with hopelessness, worry, and fear that you lose sight of your path. Suddenly, the path doesn't seem so clear. Suddenly, all the progress that has been made seems so insignificant now. The bright and lit path now seems so dim. I understood this as saying trials will come to throw you off your path or cause you to stand still and not continue to move forward. Sometimes it may even be things we do ourselves. But rest assured, that path is still there, cleared and lit up. God did not dim his light; we just lost sight. So, in this vision, as the rain falls into my eyes, my sight becomes impaired. To solve this, I put my hand over my eyes like a visor. This instantly stops the rain from bothering my sight and allows me to see clearly again, so I can continue on my path. The rain was still falling, but it no longer affected my vision or my progress in walking this path. I believe this part is telling us that you have to put on some protection when the storms of life are raging and impairing your vision and impeding your progress. You have to provide yourself protection, whether it be the Word of God, prayer, or talking with someone who can uplift and encourage you. What's going to be that hand over your eyes? What's going to be that visor that protects your sight? Please don't let doubt, fear, anxiety, or depression detour or stop you. Remember, those are just elements that come to cause distraction and delay. Your path is already made for you, and God has cleared it and made it SEEN. Now your job is to walk it and keep your eyes clear from the elements of life that may come at you by providing yourself protection and direction from the Word of God and through prayer.

Coming back to the subject of hope and considering the importance of the Word of God in our lives, I would like to look at one of my favorite scriptures to help us understand what hope is. Romans 8:24-25 NIV "But hope that is seen is no hope at all. For who hopes for what he sees? But if we hope for what we do not see, we wait for it with patience." This verse tells us that hope is hoping for what you do not have or see in front of you. The ending of that verse also informs us that we are to hope and patiently wait for it. Those few words say a lot to me. "Wait for it," this phrase reminds me of something I would say to my kids. I picture my child asking me for a peanut butter and jelly sandwich, and I reply, "Ok buddy, I'll make you one." And as I'm making it, he calls out again, "Mommy, I want a sandwich, please." To which I reply, "Be patient and wait." Or "It's in the process," "It's coming," or "I'm about to give it to you." Do you see where I'm going with this? Why would you tell someone to wait for it patiently if you never intended to provide it? Can you grasp it now? We are to hope and wait in expectation for it, to be confident we will receive it, confident God is providing it and that it is on its way. To be fully persuaded that it's yours! My Friends, understand that hope pushes you towards manifestation. It is the driving force that carries you to your victory. How, you ask? The positive mindset that hope brings can motivate you to take action toward achieving your goals and manifesting your dreams into reality. Once you take action, the thing "not seen" that you hoped for is now manifested and right in front of you. So, hope for the things you want to have or see and wait patiently for it to happen. Furthermore, faith and hope go hand in hand. You can't have Faith without hope, and you can't have hope without faith. According to scripture, this is true. Hebrews 11:1 NLT states: "Faith shows the reality [confidence] of what we hope for; it is the evidence of things we cannot see." In the KJV translation, it states that "Faith is the substance of things hoped for." Substance is interpreted as "a setting under or support," and hope can be defined as "the confident expectation of something good or something you desire coming your way." So, let's break that down. Faith is the support or the firm foundation for that which you confidently expect and desire to come your way. So, if faith is a support or foundation, then it needs something to support to be fully effective. Faith needs hope to be fully effective in its purpose. Did you get that? Just in case you don't get it yet, allow me to make it more relatable and personify it. I imagine this as someone who is trying to reach something above them but is just not quite tall enough. They need something they can stand on that can support them so they can reach it. Something sturdy and firm so that they won't fall. Hope is the person not quite tall enough, and Faith is the supporting object they can use to stand on to reach. To put it simply, Faith is a supporter of your hope. An unshakable firm foundation that your hope can be built on. I hope this is speaking to you as it is me! My dear readers, do not think you can go on a journey of hope without faith. You need both to see a positive change! We were all given a measure of faith, as said in Romans 12:3. It's up to us what we choose to do with that measure of faith. Maybe we should take a minute to look into the definition of Faith. From the dictionary, you will see it defined as "complete trust or confidence in someone or something." It can also be interpreted as "belief." In the Bible, the Greek word for Faith is Pistis. If you look up the definition of this Greek word, you will find a few definitions, but the ones that stick out to me are assurance and persuasion. The word "assurance" can be defined as "confident." So, if we combine the words "confident" and "persuaded," we get "confidently persuaded." From these two words, we can translate it to one of my favorite phrases to describe faith, "fully persuaded." Being fully persuaded comes by believing that what the Lord has said to us, He will surely bring to pass! I believe that being fully persuaded can be similar to how confidently sure you are that when you flip a light switch, you fully expect it to come on. Or how about when you get in your car and turn it on and expect it to start without any doubt in your mind. That is faith, my friends, and if we can have this undoubting, confident faith in these material things, then why not in the creator of this world? The Bible also mentions that without Faith it is impossible to please God. I believe we can all agree that pleasing God is our ultimate goal, so we all need to understand the great importance of having faith. Please understand that both faith and hope require action. It is not enough to simply say, "I hope this, and this will happen for me," without putting your faith into it and then some action behind your faith. We can't just say we believe for something and then sit back and do nothing. Faith without works is dead, right? This concept is found in the book of James, where the author writes, "What good is it, my brothers and sisters, if someone claims to have faith but has no deeds? Can such faith save them...faith by itself, if it is not accompanied by action, is dead" (James 2:14-17, NIV). I love the interpretation of the AMP translation of this scripture. It says, "No, a mere claim of faith is not sufficient—genuine faith produces good works." It also gives an example to explain this concept in verses 15-16. It states that if you see someone who is without adequate clothing and lacks enough food for each day, and you say to them, "Go in peace with my blessing, keep warm and feed yourselves," but you do not give them the necessities for the body, what good does that do? So too, faith, if it does not have works to back it up, is by itself dead [inoperative and ineffective]. And in case we still didn't get it, it provides another example of someone allowing his faith and actions to work together. In verse 21-23 it talks of Abraham and how he was justified by his works or "actions" when he offered his son Isaac on the altar as a sacrifice to God. His "action" was his obedience which expressed his faith, and his faith was working together with his action, and as a result of the action, his faith was completed. So, what does this mean for us today? It means that simply believing in something is not enough. Our actions must reflect our beliefs, or else they are meaningless. So, if you want to escape a state of hopelessness and better your life, it will take more than just wanting to restore your hope and faith; it will require you to take action. It will require you to stop speaking and thinking negatively and cultivate a language and mindset of positivity over yourself and your life. It will require you to get into the word of God daily so that your faith may not fail but be strengthened. It will require you to change your surroundings from those who live in negativity and nurse your negativity to those who live in positivity and will help pull you out. It will require you to stop making excuses and make better use of your time. It will require you to research affirmations to speak over yourself daily until you believe them. It may require you to post scriptures of God's promises on your walls so that you are reminded of his promises over your life every day. I think you get the point now. Without action, your hope and faith will be meaningless, and you will remain stagnant. So, as you activate your hope and faith today, don't forget to take action!

Maybe you're asking, "How do I cultivate hope in my life?" "Where do I even start?" Those are great questions, and there are several things you can do, but here are a few that really helped me. First, focus on the positive aspects of your life, no matter how small they may seem. Recognize and celebrate your achievements, and be grateful for the blessings you have in your life. Take the time to speak them out loud. Also, remember it's not about what you may presently feel. Don't go by what you feel; go by the facts and the truth. Secondly, set both short-term and long-term realistic goals for yourself, and work towards them with purpose and determination. Setting realistic goals is important because it gives you something to work towards and helps you stay motivated. Thirdly, as mentioned above, surround yourself with positive people who can inspire and uplift you and who will push you to reach your goals. As a matter of fact, I DARE you to do it! I dare you to allow positive people to speak into your life who have faith out of this world, drive, and determination and who will push you to create a life of positivity. Do it, and watch how beautifully your life will change. I promise you; this is one of the most important steps! It is also essential to practice self-care. Taking care of yourself physically, emotionally, and mentally is vital to cultivating a life of hope, and it is a great approach to avoid burnout. Get enough sleep, eat healthy, take time for activities that you enjoy, and reward yourself! If you ever need ideas for self-care, utilize Google, as they have numerous ideas! Another important step is developing a growth mindset. A growth mindset is the belief that you can learn and grow from challenges and setbacks. So, instead of seeing failures as evidence of your limitations, see them as opportunities to learn, improve, and grow. And finally, never give up on your dreams, no matter how far-fetched they may seem. Remember, hope is the fuel that keeps us moving forward, even in the face of adversity. I want to encourage you to hold on to hope. Don't believe the lies of the enemy. Don't let the negativity in your mind and thoughts control you. Believe that things can change and that there is a brighter future waiting for you. Know that you have the strength and resilience to get through whatever challenges you are facing right now. Stand firm and strong in your hope and faith, and watch what God will do with it. "Rejoice in hope, be patient in tribulation, be constant in prayer" Romans 12:12. And remember that you are not alone; there are people around you who care and want to support you.

Reflective Questions

1. How can experiencing hopelessness impact your mental, emotional, and physical well-being?

2. What are some potential sources of hopelessness in your life, and how can you prevent yourself from entering that state?

3. How does having hope provide you with motivation, purpose, and direction in your life, even during challenging times?

PRAYER

Dear Heavenly Father,
Thank you for the power of Hope in my life. In a world that often experiences hopelessness, help me to recognize the importance of cultivating and maintaining hope in my heart. I pray that You will protect me from falling into hopelessness by Your grace and mercy. As I seek You and meditate on Your promises, I pray that You guide me and make my path clear. Help me to trust in your unchanging nature and believe that you are leading me to my purpose. Grant me wisdom to put up a shield against doubt, fear, anxiety, and depression. May I find protection and direction in your Word and through prayer. I pray that You cultivate in me a spirit of patient expectation, trusting that what I hope for will manifest according to Your perfect timing. Let me remember that I must take action to see the change I desire. Thank you for the gift of hope, Lord. Help me to hold onto it tightly, even in the face of adversity. May hope be the driving force that propels me toward manifestation and victory.
In Jesus Name, Amen.

CHAPTER 3

SURROUNDINGS AND SEASONS

Who and what are you surrounding yourself with? This is a great question to ask when you find yourself feeling hopeless and stuck in motion. I remember hearing someone speak about how your surroundings have a lot to do with how you feel and think about life and view things in life. As I pondered that idea, I reflected on my life during my time of hopelessness and wondered if it could apply to me. As I recalled "what" I was surrounding myself with at that time, I realized that I spent much of my day watching tv shows that were either completely unrealistic or maybe close to reality, but not my life. Shows that would have me feeling dissatisfied with my current life and wishing for something different. It became evident that I was not surrounding myself with positivity or anything beneficial to my mental health. Don't get me wrong; I am not against television at all. However, as time went on, I found myself feeling an increased sense of hopelessness as my leisure time was consumed by a state of stagnation. In all reality, wasting time on meaningless things is just another way to suppress and avoid our emotions. At least for me, it was. I never intended to waste my time watching TV. In fact, I would get so angry at myself for wasting time when I could have been doing more productive things. But honestly, that's the tricky part about hopelessness and depression. You know you should be doing something more productive with your time, but you have no energy, motivation, or drive to do it. I would also spend numerous hours on social media, getting sucked into the rabbit holes. We all know social media platforms have a way of getting you to escape the real life in front of you, right? We see these seemingly picture-perfect lives as we scroll through pictures and videos, believing the facades that others post of the picture-perfect tidy house and lifestyle, where it's nothing but peace, sunshine, and rainbows. And we then get sucked in. Sucked into thinking we are not good enough or our lives are not good enough because our life doesn't look like theirs. While getting sucked into this miserable place called comparison, we forget to understand that everything is not as it seems. We often only see a small portion of their lives or accomplishments and may not be aware of the challenges or setbacks they have faced or are facing. We must remember that no one on this earth is without trouble or hard times. Absolutely no one is exempt. Comparison is one of the most dangerous devices that can lead you into a state of hopelessness. How, you may ask? It can lead to feelings of inadequacy and low self-esteem and distort your perception of reality, which in turn, can cause a state of depression. Speaking from experience, comparison is a dangerous game to play, my friends. Comparison is a distraction. It can keep you from walking the specific path that God has laid out before you toward your purpose in life. I urge you to grasp reality and remind yourself that no life is perfect or without trouble and hardships, and kick comparison out of your mind and your life for good! There is absolutely no room for comparison in the journey to great mental health.

As I reflected on "who" I chose to surround myself with, I took a close look at my surroundings and realized that many of the people around me at this time displayed a sense of complacency. While I couldn't say for certain what their internal thoughts and feelings were, I never heard them express any desire to pursue new goals or experiences. In fact, I never heard them speak with excitement about life, their future, or their dreams. When we would gather, we would mainly talk about the challenges we faced and the many hardships of life. It occurred to me that at this time in my life, I had never really been in the company of people who were hopeful or enthusiastic about life. During this time of introspection, I also realized I was stuck in a repetitive daily cycle. I never really did things out of the ordinary or tried something different to give myself a break from the repetitiveness of my days. I'm sure we all can attest that being on a repetitive day-to-day schedule will have us feeling weary and hopeless sooner or later. At this time, I was active in ministry at my church and had been in a leadership role for five years. What I did not realize at the time was that the ministry started to become a part of my repetitive cycle. Without saying too much, I noticed that even though I was in a God-centered environment, my surrounding was not conducive to encouraging one to find their God-given purpose in life or to follow dreams they may have for their life. I realized I viewed purpose as actively doing something for the Kingdom of God inside the walls of the church, as this is what my surroundings believed. My surroundings influenced me to believe that any ministry you are in inside the church is your purpose from God. But why did I feel so hopeless? Why did I feel stuck and somewhat empty? I remember feeling so confused and guilty for feeling incomplete when I was clearly in active ministry, which is my purpose, right? Or was it? Was I simply living up to someone else's expectations of my purpose? Was this why I felt incomplete? I realized I had never really sought guidance from God regarding my purpose. In fact, I didn't fully understand what purpose meant. I relied on what man defined as purpose instead of seeking it from the one who creates a unique purpose for each and every one of us. I believe this is why I felt unfulfilled and stuck. Now don't get me wrong, I definitely believe your purpose can be the ministry you are actively in, but I do not condone the belief that it is the only area your purpose can be in. Purpose can manifest in various forms throughout our lives. Through this time in my life, I learned a great lesson; you have to be careful not to give man, or your surroundings, too much influence over your thoughts and beliefs. Doing so may cause you to minimize or ignore your own inclinations and beliefs and forget to seek the creator who assigns purpose himself!

So, what exactly does purpose mean? Or better yet, what do I personally define as purpose? Glad you asked. You can find an all-around meaning of purpose as the reason or intention behind something. I personally feel that purpose is the driving force that motivates and guides our actions and gives meaning and direction to our lives. I also believe that finding your purpose can be a key factor in achieving fulfillment, happiness, and a sense of well-being. Discovering or understanding one's purpose is a challenge that many people face, and I strongly believe that it stems from a lack of understanding regarding the true meaning of purpose and how to find it. To grasp the concept of purpose, one thing you must understand is that it is not limited to one thing. You can hold multiple purposes throughout your life. Your purpose can manifest at different times in various areas, such as relationships, career, personal growth, contributions to society, and spiritual fulfillment, just to name a few. Let's explore the concept of purpose and how we can discover it. One way to uncover your purpose is by looking deep into your heart and your desires in life and asking yourself, "What gives me meaning and direction for my life? What makes me feel motivated when I think about it?" Or maybe ask yourself, "If I could do anything I dreamed or thought about, what would it be?" Perhaps it would be a dream to write a book one day. Or writing a tv series or movie. Maybe speaking hope and positivity into others is something that motivates you when thinking about it. Maybe it's serving others, whether serving the homeless community or possibly serving through your own food service like a restaurant or food truck. Perhaps it could be helping your community with services for tutoring underprivileged kids who may be struggling. It could be starting a new career you've always dreamed of doing. These are just a few examples to help you start thinking outside of the box. Ask yourself these questions in the mindset that money isn't a worry. Once you bring in the mindset of "But I don't have the resources," it immediately limits your idea and reality of your purpose. Listen, your faith can conform to your reality, or your reality can conform to your faith. This is such a great statement made by my Pastor that really makes you think, and I don't know about you, but I choose the second! Why not trust God to show you your purpose and have faith it will be your reality? The God we serve, who creates purpose, is not limited in any way. He owns all the resources; he reigns and rules over all the Earth. He can cause things to come to pass before we even ask. In the words of my Pastor, "If you don't recognize God properly, then you won't see your purpose clearly." He went on to explain how God has designs or plans for our life that are greater than we can believe about ourselves. So, if you limit God's designs or plans by what you think you are capable of, then you will always have a limited perception of what you can accomplish, but when you begin to see God for who he is and see you how He sees you, you will be able to believe what you can become. He continued to encourage that you can rest in the reality that God has chosen you, and there is a purpose for who you are. He also emphasized that you owe it to yourself to find out who you're meant to be, and you owe it to the God that designed you to become all that you can be! Second Timothy 1:9-10 AMP states: "He delivered us and saved us and called us with a holy calling [a calling that leads to a consecrated life—a life set apart—a life of purpose], not because of our works [or because of any personal merit—we could do nothing to earn this], but because of His own purpose and grace [His amazing, undeserved favor] which was granted to us in Christ Jesus before the world began." There is a big world out there waiting for you to find your purpose and shine in it. I implore you; please don't limit yourself! I can confidently speak on this because I am living proof of the outcome that can come from asking yourself these questions and trusting God to help you as you pursue them. Although my full testimony will come in the latter part of this book, I want to encourage all who are reading that finding your purpose is not as hard as it may seem. Just this simple act of asking yourself these questions will begin to open your mind to help you find the purpose in life you want to go after. Don't forget to start by seeking God and praying for guidance. Ask God to reveal His plan to you, and then ask yourself the above questions. Listen carefully, as God will speak to you.

I want to talk about a lost art mentioned above that I'm committed to reviving, and I plan on passing it down to my children and anyone else who wants to hear. This "lost art" is the ability and understanding to hear God's voice for yourself. I say it's a lost art because, about two years ago, I realized I was never properly taught or empowered to discern and hear the voice of God for myself, and I have been in church since I was born. Unfortunately, this seems to be a common multi-generational issue among many leaders. Throughout my life, I have been a member of a few churches, but only recently did I truly receive guidance on how to discern and hear the voice of God. Due to this lack of teaching, I had always relied on the man or woman of God who was preaching to provide me with a word from God specifically for my life. I remember being in services with known prophets hoping and praying they would approach me with a message from God. Had I ever asked him to speak directly to me? No, I had not. Not because I didn't believe God could speak to me directly but because, as mentioned above, I was never taught how to listen for, discern, or hear the voice of God. I see now that I was in a place of dependency on man and not God. We must be careful not to exalt man over God, even mistakenly. While I fully believe a man/woman of God can speak a word into your life, I now know that is not the extent of it. We are to seek God for ourselves and commune with him. What happens in communication? There's dialogue from both sides, correct? Prayer is not for you to do all the talking and then allow God no time to speak to you. I am a witness that if you seek him and ask him to communicate with you, he will indeed do that. How do I know when it's God, you may ask? Understand He can speak with inspirations, dreams, visions, an overwhelming feeling you may have, words that come to your mind that you may be thinking repeatedly, or a word you may say in conversation, and your spirit is immediately stirred. He can also speak to you from the Word of God (the Bible) as you read it. It can also be audible words you may hear so loud and clear. The key is knowing his voice. We can gather the inspiration from the scriptures concerning the passage in John chapter 10 that states the sheep know the shepherd's voice and how they correlate it to knowing God's voice in your life. I've been in the place where I questioned, "God, is this you, or is this me?" I prayed and asked God to let me know his voice from all others. I want to know his voice more clearly than I know my husband's, parents, siblings, or my children's. When you connect with God in prayer and earnestly seek after his voice, I am a witness that he will respond, and you will begin to KNOW his voice in your life. For example, after I became familiar with the various ways in which the Holy Spirit communicates, I began to set aside a specific time during my prayers when I just intently listened. Many times, while listening, there will be words that come to my mind that are positive and encouraging, and I know that it is him speaking to me. There are times when I will ask God something specific, and after I ask, I will meditate and be silent. And so many times in that quiet moment, he will bring a specific scripture or bible passage to my mind, and as I look into it, something from the passage will jump out at me, and I will hear a specific word from that passage. I also began asking God to communicate with me in my dreams while I sleep. God answered, and I've had quite a few dreams of him communicating with me, and they have been nothing short of amazing! I want to encourage you in this moment to seek after the voice of God in your life. He never intended our communication to be one-sided. This is true based on the way in which God created man and openly interacted with him in the beginning. I honestly believe that with all the distractions we have in this day and time, it makes it harder for us to focus and meditate after we speak to God. However, you can find his voice/words if you make an effort to listen. I promise you it's there. You just have to be intentional about it. "Ask, and it will be given to you; seek, and you will find; knock, and it will be opened to you. For everyone who asks receives, and the one who seeks finds, and to the one who knocks it will be opened." Matthew 7:7-8 ESV.

SEASONS

I was talking to a friend one day, and we began to talk about the mental state of people today. As we discussed it, I said, "I truly believe a major factor in depression and the negative mental state of most people today is because they feel stuck." As I ponder that thought, it really makes sense. When you feel stuck, like there's no upward/forward movement for you, what is typically your reaction? Maybe, you get overwhelmed and then discouraged to the point that you do nothing. Honestly, this is a very common response for most people when they feel stuck in life. It's easy to do nothing and give up. However, this response can lead you to a point where you begin to lose hope, and your faith starts to dwindle. As a result, your mindset becomes negative, and you now decide to swallow the hopeless pill, letting it dissolve and release into your innermost being. Now, because of this release and overtaking, you're swept away by depression, and it all began because you believed a lie that you're STUCK where you are. Yes, I said a lie. A lie you maybe told yourself. Maybe a lie the enemy whispered in your ear. Or perhaps a lie you believed due to what you were surrounded by or going through. But oh, how quickly we forget about seasons! What if I told you that feeling stuck is just a season of life and that seasons always change? By nature, we know that seasons in the natural have an end, right? Well, my friends, so in the spiritual! SEASONS CHANGE! Think about the changing of seasons in nature. Each season has its own unique beauty, but it also has its challenges. Summer can be hot and uncomfortable, but it can also allow so many beautiful flowers and fruits to grow that only come in this season. Winter can be cold and dreary, but it can bring forth the prettiest scenery of blankets of white snow. So, in the challenges of summer, do we sit in our house and refuse to come out because it's too hot and seems like it will never end? Or do we go on with our lives and say, "Man, I can't stand this heat! I can't wait for Fall!"

The latter, right? What did we do there? We "HOPED" for Fall, a new season. We believe that once the season changes to Fall, it will bring cooler weather and relieve our current misery or discomfort. We have an expectation that something better is going to come to us with the change of the season! Again, I say, as in the natural, so in the spiritual. Friends, I'm here to tell you that you will not be stuck in a season forever! You need to hope and wait patiently for your new season of refreshing to come.

Can we quickly take a moment and consider Job in the bible? What about Joseph? Job went through a season of suffering, but in the end, he was blessed with twice as much as he had before. Joseph went through a season of betrayal and imprisonment, but he eventually rose to a position of power and influence. Not only did their season change, it changed for the BETTER. When their season changed, they came into their purpose and favor! We, too, can come out of a tough season stronger and better than before. It's all about our mindset and how we approach the situation. This is something we must diligently remind ourselves of so that we can escape the previously stated mudslide of hopelessness. You may be asking yourself, why am I facing so many challenges in this season? This is a reasonable question. Even Job and possibly Joseph asked this question. Based on the passages describing their experience during their dark season, it is evident that they were feeling low and defeated, maybe even considered hopeless at some point. While Joseph's story doesn't specifically state if he ever asked the above question or felt hopeless, it does provide insight into his emotional journey, which leads me to the conclusion mentioned above. However, after Job had conversations with friends that went nowhere and seemed to make his misery worse, he finally had a conversation with God that brought him out of his season of misery into his new season of promise and purpose. Joseph's hope dwindled as days continued to go by and turned into years, and he was still stuck in prison after begging the two other prisoners to put in a good word for him. As he realized they had forgotten him, he finally had to relinquish his hope in man and fully rely on his hope in God. Once he did, his season changed for the better. We can also gather from these two examples that, as in the words of my pastor, God is more concerned about building our character than making us happy. It is his job to help us develop our character to one that is comparable to his and one that will position us to be able to walk in our purpose. So, if we can view these seasons as steps towards our divine purpose and the next season of better, then we will be able to get through the challenges of the current season without feeling stuck and without giving up.

Scripture reminds us in John 10:10, that God's purpose is to give us a rich and satisfying life. So, what is the recipe for avoiding the feeling of being stuck in a dark season? Keep your eyes on the season change that's coming! Conversate with God, fill your mind with his promises, and hope only in Him! Instead of giving up, we must hold onto hope and remember that this too shall pass. We need to remember the promises of God and trust that he has a plan for our lives. "Every day isn't going to be perfect, but it doesn't mean it doesn't have a purpose!" -Pastor Robert Tisdale. So, the next time you feel stuck or things get uncomfortable, hard, or even miserable. That is not the time to hang up your hope and sulk in sorrow. That is your time to remember the promises of God and to remember that this is just a season, and this season will come to an end, and a new season will arise. We await the end of the current season and hope for the new season coming. Who knows, it may just be your best one yet!

Surroundings Reflective Questions

1. What are the negative influences or distractions in your life that contribute to feelings of hopelessness and stagnation?

2. What role do your surroundings play in shaping your feelings about life and your view of the world?

3. Are you seeking your purpose based on external influences and societal expectations, or are you taking the time to understand your own desires, motivations, and the voice of God within you?

Surroundings Prayer

Dear Heavenly Father,
I come before you with a humble heart. Help me, Lord, to be mindful of the influences in my life. Forgive me for seeking fulfillment in meaningless things and for comparing my life to others. I pray for the wisdom to understand that no one's life is without trouble or hardship. Help me to let go of comparison and embrace my own journey, knowing that You have a unique purpose for me. Guide me to discover what truly motivates and inspires me, and grant me the courage to pursue it. Teach me, Lord, to hear Your voice clearly. I long to deepen my relationship with You and to discern Your guidance in my life. Open my ears and my heart to listen attentively. I surrender my surroundings and my desires to You, Lord. Fill me with hope and enthusiasm for life, and surround me with people who encourage and uplift me. May my choices align with Your purpose for me, bringing fulfillment, joy, and a sense of well-being. Thank you for your unfailing love and grace. I commit to seeking You first and trusting in Your plans for my life.
In Jesus name, Amen.

Seasons Reflective Questions

1. When faced with challenges or a feeling of being stuck, what are some negative reactions or behaviors you tend to exhibit? How do these responses contribute to a sense of hopelessness?

2. Reflecting on the changing seasons in nature, how can you adopt a mindset of hope and anticipation for the next season in your own life? How does this perspective help you navigate difficult situations and maintain a positive outlook?

3. Are you relying more on human support and solutions rather than placing your hope and trust in God during challenging times? How can you deepen your relationship with God and lean on His promises to navigate through seasons of darkness?

Prayer

Dear Heavenly Father,
Thank you for the power of hope and the promise of change. Help me to have the right perspective, Lord. Just as I eagerly await the change of seasons in nature, let me also eagerly anticipate the new season in my life. Give me the strength to hold on to hope and to patiently wait for the refreshing that comes with a new season. In moments of doubt and despair, remind me to turn to You, Lord. Help me to fill my mind with Your promises. Let me always remember that your Word is a source of encouragement and strength during challenging times. I pray that I will never lose sight of Your faithfulness and the rich and satisfying life You desire for me. Father, I ask for a mindset shift. Help me to see these challenging seasons as opportunities for growth and character development. Align my heart with Your will and guide me on the path that leads to my purpose. Remind me that every day has a purpose. Thank You, Lord, for Your faithfulness and for the assurance that this current season will pass. I eagerly await the new season that You have prepared for me. May Your grace and peace be with me as I navigate the challenges of life and cling to the hope of a better tomorrow.
In Jesus Name, Amen.

CHAPTER 4

CHANGING THE NARRATIVE

We can all acknowledge that life sometimes presents us with uncomfortable, frightening, and even traumatic situations or experiences. It is usually in these moments that these experiences leave a lasting negative impact on our lives. In this chapter, I want to share a strategy to help you change the way you view these experiences so that they no longer negatively affect or control you. I know for me personally, I've had a fair share of uncomfortable and traumatic moments in my life that have definitely negatively affected me and, to some extent, controlled me. Honestly, more than I care for. In the first chapter of this book, I briefly shared some of my experiences. However, for the sake of transparency, I will provide additional details. One of the traumatic experiences I endured was when my body was struck by a severe bacterial infection that truly rocked my world. Not only did it horribly affect my body, but it also brought on a horrible mental illness as well. I developed crippling anxiety from this traumatic experience that greatly limited my life and life experiences. About a year later, my body was healing well, and I was able to have my first child. He was the greatest gift I had ever received, but little did I know the anxiety would only get worse. I tried to ignore it and push it down to the best of my ability. I even stayed in the house as often as possible, so I didn't have to deal with it as much. Then came my second traumatic experience after the birth of my second child. Basically, after giving birth, there were some complications. These complications would also magnify the state of anxiety I was already in. I then went through the dreaded PPD (post-partum depression). When I say scary, I mean it was scary. If you've ever been in a state where you felt you didn't have control of your body or your mind, then you will understand this type of scary. Although I suffered for many years from anxiety and the memories of the traumatic experiences and allowed them to control my mental and physical state. I can stand here today, ten years later, and say I am now delivered from it all. All due to the mercy and grace of God and the hard work I had to put in, which included changing the narrative of how I viewed my traumatic experiences. I am so grateful I am free today! And good news, you can be too! I'm going to share with you some things throughout this chapter that will help you apply this concept of "changing the narrative."

Going through an old journal, I found a selection I wrote that I feel is perfect for this concept of "changing the narrative." Please forgive me, as I cannot remember the source of the information found in this journal entry. However, it was a concept to ask yourself three questions when you find yourself in rough patches in life and when times are hard. Instead of asking "Why?" they suggest that these three questions would be a more beneficial way to work through those tough times. The first question is, "How have your priorities changed for the better?" This question helps us to see, when up against a challenge that truly shakes us to the core, what's really important in life. Once we acknowledge the priority shift, it puts the important things into perspective and draws us closer to those most important things in life. The second question is, "What positive qualities in yourself have been brought to the surface?" This question will allow us to take notice of our own strength, love, bravery, and passion, which we often don't realize we have until we are put to the test. I think we can all attest that we've experienced a scary time in our lives that we got through, even though we were probably scared to our core. When put in these serious situations, we often find strength and courage we didn't even know we possessed. And pointing them out through this question can help you change the narrative of that awful experience! The third and final question asks, "What are you learning now (through this experience) that will serve you in the future?" See, the insights that become available when we persevere through our struggles stay with us for years to come. If we can extract some positivity from those tough times, they can often make us more equipped to handle future hardships. Learning through our tough experiences is incredibly beneficial to us for the present and the future. We can also be of benefit to others who might be going through something similar. I recall a time in my life when I used this strategy, and it greatly helped me. My youngest son had an allergic reaction to a food he ate. Once I saw the rash forming around his mouth, I quickly got the Benadryl and gave it to him. I nervously watched him for the next few minutes to see if any other reactions would come. Sure enough, he begins coughing. After giving him some water, he explained that it was hard to swallow it. I immediately loaded him up in the car and headed to the closest urgent care. On the drive, I was literally shaking and trembling in fear, worried that his throat would close up. However, I knew I had to keep it together for him so that he did not freak out. So, with all my strength, I smiled and calmly told him, "You're going to be ok, baby. We're just going to get you checked out. Everything is ok; just keep talking to Mommy." Even though everything inside of me wanted to break down and succumb to the anxiousness and fear I was feeling, I was able to be strong and brave for him. Long story short, we got there, and he got what he needed, and everything turned out fine. Thank God! Even though I was greatly relieved, all those emotions racing through my body all at once and all the negative thoughts that tried to overtake me in those moments left me weary and burdened. As I came home, I went up to my room and let out a good cry. As I began talking to the Lord, I felt an urge to "change the narrative". These questions above came to my mind, and I decided to try them. As I asked myself these questions, I realized just how strong I was and how capable I was to remain strong and in control for my son in that intense moment. Despite being overwhelmed by anxiety that threatened to cripple both my body and mind, I was able to conquer and overcome it and get my child to safety. With this newfound understanding, I turned my tears of sorrow into tears of joy. Although I would have rather not had to go through that experience, I can now see my inner strength and capability in scary situations and use it as a reminder during future hardships. I also realized through asking myself the first question that everything I had planned for that day no longer mattered, and it allowed me to see that my priorities were in the right place.

Through my life experiences, I have come to realize that the challenges we face are not always meant solely for ourselves. This realization became even more apparent to me as I wrote this book. I often questioned God, asking why I had to endure so many traumatic events and their aftermath. However, as I began to share with others my experiences and how I overcame them, I saw that my story provided hope and inspiration to those going through similar struggles. This made me realize that the victories I achieved were not just for me but were to uplift and encourage others. And for that reason, I cannot silence my voice. For in these moments, God has allowed me to be his servant and help his beloved people. What I thought would bring me down and possibly kill me proved to be a blessing not just for me but for others too! These events not only showed me how strong and able I am with God to come out of said trials, but they also continue to bless me and bring me joy every time I tell my testimony, and it helps someone else come out in victory. I am reminded of the scripture in Jeremiah 29:11 that states, "For I know the plans I have for you," declares the LORD, "plans to prosper you and not to harm you, plans to give you hope and a future." I never would've imagined that the hardest, scariest, and most challenging times in my life would bring me joy. But oh, how God turns it around for our good! I am thankful to be a witness of his goodness today.

I've come to understand that rewiring your thought process about your negative or traumatic experiences is incredibly important to maintain your hope and peace of mind. As a matter of fact, not only to "maintain," but sometimes rewiring is required to "obtain" hope and peace of mind. That means if your circumstances have you doubting, worrying, or spiraling into negativity, you need to quickly change the narrative. Although sometimes we may not have any control over certain circumstances in our lives, we do have control over what narrative we allow our mind to create and perceive. Take that control and use it! For instance, if your mind is trying to tell you that you're going to miss important moments in life because of the circumstance you are experiencing. Rewire your mind to think of how many moments you are going to make once you come out of said experience. In simpler words, find the positive! Allow the narrative you create in your mind to carry you to hope and peace. Romans 15:13 "May the God of hope fill you with all joy and peace in believing, so that by the power of the Holy Spirit you may abound in hope."

Reflective Questions

1. How can changing the narrative of your negative or traumatic experiences lead to obtaining hope and peace of mind?

2. In what ways have your past traumatic experiences served as a source of strength and inspiration for you or others in need of hope?

3. How can rewiring your thought process and controlling the narrative in your mind help you find joy and peace even in the midst of difficult circumstances?

Prayer

Dear Heavenly Father,
I thank you for your presence in my life, knowing that you are always with me, offering comfort and strength. I seek to change the way I view my challenging experiences. Help me, Lord, to reroute my thoughts and take control of my personal narratives. I lay at your feet the scary and traumatic moments of my life, knowing that you are my refuge and source of healing. I release them and the negativity they bring into my life. May these experiences become stepping stones toward growth and maturity. Equip me to handle future hardships with grace, drawing strength from the lessons I have learned. Show me the strength, resilience, and courage that reside within me. Help me to recognize my own capabilities, even when I feel overwhelmed and afraid. I ask for Your guidance in rewiring my thought processes. When negativity and doubt threaten to overwhelm me, help me to quickly change the narrative. Give me the ability to find the positive in every situation and to hold onto hope and peace of mind. May my heart be filled with gratitude for the blessings I have, even in the midst of difficulties. May you fill me with all joy and peace in believing, so that by the power of the Holy Spirit, I may abound in hope. I trust in your plans for me, plans to prosper me and give me a future filled with hope.
In Jesus Name, Amen.

CHAPTER 5

TRANSFORMATION

It's important to keep in mind that negative thoughts and feelings can create a cycle of negativity that can keep you stuck in a state of hopelessness. Transformation is vital, specifically the transformation of the mind. In the words of Pastor Robert Tisdale, "Transformation starts in your mind before it shows on the outside. What we focus on, we attract. What we think about, we manifest." Understand that at some point, your thoughts will become your actions, and your actions will become your habits. So basically, if you want to change your life, you have to start by changing or transforming the way that you think. Proverbs 23:7 "For as he thinketh in his heart, so is he."

In the word of God, Romans 12:2 tells us, "Be not conformed to this world: but be ye transformed by the renewing of your mind, that ye may prove what is that good, and acceptable, and perfect, will of God." Renewing your mind is about filling your mind with God's truth and allowing it to transform you from the inside out. I believe it means letting go of old ways of thinking that are holding you back and embracing a new way of thinking that is aligned with God's will for your life. It could also be explained as interpreting life through the lens of God's word rather than the lens of your experience, trauma, or preferences. If you are conformed to the world's ways of thinking and not God's, do not be fooled into thinking you are connected to him and his will. We are called to renew our minds in Him because it will cause a transformation, which will be followed by a connection to God that we will be able to know and walk in his will for us. But here's the thing, renewing your mind is not a one-time event. It's a daily commitment and a daily process of growth and transformation. Colossians 3:10 AMP says, "Put on the new [spiritual] self who is being continually renewed in true knowledge in the image of Him." This shows us that transformation is continual, and you have to be intentional about it. You have to be intentional about filling your mind with positivity and doing things that will encourage your growth, like reading the word of God, praying, speaking affirmations, and doing it continually. The Bible says in Philippians 4:8 NLT to "Fix your thoughts on what is true, and honorable, and right, and pure, and lovely, and admirable. Think about things that are excellent and worthy of praise." Pay attention to the first two words of this mentioned text, "Fix your." These two words alone imply that this is something YOU have to do. In the previous chapter, we discussed how faith requires you to take action. However, we can see from the word of God that transformation requires action as well. The Bible also records in Colossians 3:1-2 to "seek the things that are above" and "set your mind on things above." Again, a call to action for transformation. Most of Colossians chapter three speaks about transformation from an old self to a new self. I really love how the message translation of Colossians 3:9-14 compares this passage to a wardrobe analogy. It mentions how the old you/life is like a filthy set of ill-fitting clothes that you need to strip off and put into the fire. But now that you are in Christ, your new self/life is like a new wardrobe, where every item is custom-made by the Creator with his label on it. So, what is this transformed wardrobe God custom-made for you? It's compassion, kindness, humility, strength, discipline, forgiveness, hope, peace, joy, and love. Everything you will need to live an overcoming life. It is solely up to us to wake up every day and choose what wardrobe we are going to wear. Will you choose the filthy, ill-fitting, old wardrobe that keeps you out of alignment with God and your purpose? Or the new, custom-fit, made-by-God wardrobe that gives you all you need to succeed? Will you choose to put on peace or anxiousness? Strength or weakness? Joy or sadness? Hope or hopelessness? It's YOUR choice! We've been given the new wardrobe, but the question is, will we choose to put it on?

As mentioned above, the transformation of the mind takes you being intentional about it. Maybe you want to know of some ways to be intentional about your transformation. I will expound on some points that were previously mentioned above. You now know you need to let go of old ways of thinking and embrace a new way of thinking that is aligned with God's will. You also now know that to do that, it would help to get into the Word of God, pray, and speak affirmations. But maybe it seems easier said than done to you. And you know what? I totally get that. I've been there. As I've already mentioned, life with kids made it extremely difficult to make time for myself and to even make time for God. I can look back and say it was honestly due to my mindset. I thought my time with God had to be uninterrupted, or God would somehow not be pleased. I used to think that if my kids interrupted me while I was reading the Bible, I wouldn't be able to study effectively, and it would be a waste of time. It wasn't until I realized one day that my concept of what God would accept from me was extremely skewed. God knows exactly where we are in life and what is the best we can give in each moment of life. He is the most gracious and understanding of anyone else. So, with this newfound understanding, I began to walk my house and pray with my kids up and about. If they needed me to hold them, I would pick them up and continue to walk and pray. After a couple of weeks of doing this, they quickly caught on and left me alone when I started walking and praying. This also encouraged me because now my children could see an example of prayer. Now moving on to reading the bible, I found myself frustrated because I just didn't know where to start. When it came to studying, I didn't know what passage to choose, and if I chose one, would it be the right one or a good one? This problem probably won't make sense to someone who's not an overthinker, haha. However, I remember searching for devotionals, and I came across an article that gave a breakdown of how to do your own daily devotional. I tried it and loved it, and it honestly transformed how I study the word of God. I'm going to share it with you right now, just in case anyone else struggles in studying the word of God. First, you can open your bible app and look for the verse of the day. Before reading the verse, ask God to make you aware of anything he wants to show you. Then read through the verse, paying close attention to any words that stand out to you. (Just a side note: I like to go ahead and read the whole chapter along with the verse.) Make sure to have a journal to write in to answer the following questions.

*Compare 3-5 bible versions of this verse to give you a broader understanding of the verse.

1. What does this verse reveal to me about God's character?
2. What is the main point of this passage?
3. How can I apply this to my daily life?
4. What words or phrases stand out to me?
5. What is resonating with me?
6. How can I apply it to my life?

*Finally, you can write out 2-3 takeaways about the scripture you studied.

As I mentioned above, these tools are a part of what helped me start my transformation concerning prayer and studying the Bible. However, while studying the concept of renewing your mind, I found a great online article titled "What Does the "Renewing of the Mind" Look Like for Christians," which really goes in-depth on more ways to help you intentionally renew your mind. I want to share it with you today as I believe it will be a great help to you as it was to me. The writer of the article, Matt Tommey, mentions three "R's" to remember to effectively renew your mind to align with the truth of God's word. They are Recognize, Replace, and Reinforce. You need to recognize the lies of the enemy, replace them with the truth of God's word, and then reinforce that truth every time the enemy comes at you with those same lies. Second Corinthians 10:5 teaches us that "We destroy arguments and every lofty opinion raised against the knowledge of God, and take every thought captive to obey Christ." To take a thought captive, you need to intentionally capture it and compare it to the word of God and his promises for your life. You can ask yourself, "Does this thought line up or reflect what God's word says, or does it reflect a lie that I know doesn't represent God's heart for me?" This is the act of recognizing. If the thoughts you're having don't agree with God's word, then you need to replace them with promises from God's word. An easy way to do that is to do a quick internet search for scriptures based on the thought you are trying to replace. This is the act of replacing. I recently came across an article that claimed they did a study and found out that it takes five positive affirmations to cancel out one negative thought/word. Remember, thoughts are like seeds, and whatever you allow to be planted in your heart will bring forth a harvest in your life, so choose your seeds (thoughts) wisely. Lastly is the act of reinforcement. Every time you are flooded with those same types of thoughts that don't agree with God's best for your life, and you have rejected and replaced them, you then need to reinforce those truths through visualization and affirmations. For example, you can write down biblical affirmations on note cards and carry them with you for easy access or post them in places you often see, like your office, around your home, or in your car. For those of you who like to use your phone, I would suggest making a note of biblical affirmations and non-bible affirmations and saving it to your phone. Personally, that's what I do. It's important to not only read these affirmations but to speak them aloud. Even if you don't necessarily believe what you're saying at the moment, keep saying them because, eventually, you will come to a place where you believe them! Remember, scripture says, "Death and Life are in the power of the tongue." So, your words have the power to bring healing and restoration to your soul and mind. Simply doing these steps will allow you to come into agreement with God's design for your life, and as you do, you will be amazed at the doors that will open for you! Another thing the author pointed out was that: Renewing your mind is not just a spiritual process but a physiological one as well. When you intentionally change the way you think to align with God's Word, it literally creates new connections and pathways in your brain to make that process easier and more preferred over time. Through the process of neuroplasticity, your brain can literally be reconfigured to align with the truth of God's Word and thus create the solutions, strategies, and opportunities that best align with God's plan for your life.

Listen, the enemy knows who you are, so why don't you? He knows you're chosen and called by God, blessed and highly favored, and loved with a never-ending love. The enemy knows what that promise and purpose over your life is going to do for you and others, and he knows the great things you will do and become for God. So again, I ask, why don't you? Understand that your transformation is not just for you. Your transformation has the potential to create a ripple effect in the lives of those around you. As you embrace a positive mindset and walk boldly in your purpose, you become a beacon of hope and inspiration for others seeking their own transformation. Through the power of transformation, you can soar into your purpose, creating a legacy of love, hope, and faith for generations to come.

REFLECTIVE QUESTIONS

1. How have negative thoughts and feelings impacted your life and kept you from embracing your God-given purpose? Can you identify any specific cycles of negativity that you have experienced?

2. Based on what you've read in this chapter, what are some practical steps you can take to transform your mindset from negative to positive? What practices or habits can you implement to reinforce positive thinking and growth in your daily life?

3. As you experience the power of transformation, how can you share your journey with others and inspire them to embrace their divine purpose?

PRAYER

Dear Heavenly Father,

I come before you today with a humble heart, recognizing the power of transformation that you offer. I acknowledge that negative thoughts and emotions can keep me trapped in a state of hopelessness, but I believe that through your grace and guidance, I can experience a renewal of my mind. You have shown me that transformation starts within my mind before it manifests outwardly. Help me to focus my thoughts on what is true, honorable, right, pure, lovely, admirable, excellent, and praiseworthy. I surrender my old ways of thinking and embrace a new mindset that aligns with your perfect will for my life. I understand that renewing my mind is a daily commitment. I commit myself to fill my mind with your truth, to immerse myself in your Word, to seek you in prayer, and to speak affirmations that align with your promises. Give me the strength and discipline to engage in these practices continually. Thank you, Lord, for choosing me and calling me to a life of purpose. Help me to fully embrace this transformation and understand the impact it can have on others. May my renewed mind be a beacon of hope and inspiration, not only for myself but for those around me who are seeking their own transformation. I surrender myself to your transformative power, Lord. Mold me, shape me, and use me for your glory.
In Jesus Name, Amen.

CHAPTER 6

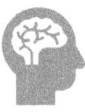

THE IMPORTANCE OF THE MIND

In this life, there is one thing that holds much power yet often remains overlooked and unappreciated. Want to take a guess what it is? If you guessed "the mind," then you are correct. The mind holds our thoughts, emotions, and perceptions and is a force that shapes our reality and molds the trajectory of our lives. Our dreams, goals, and transformations all start in our minds. The mind can either push us towards success or hold us back with self-imposed limits. In this chapter, we will explore the significance of the mind, how our thoughts affect our actions and learn simple concepts to follow to keep our mind in a healthy state.

The author of "The Road Less Traveled," M. Scott Peck, M.D., mentioned something in his book that stuck out to me so profoundly and really goes along with what is being discussed in this book. I think it stuck out to me so deeply because I've seen this happen not only in my life but in the lives of many close to me. He stated, "Neurosis is always a substitute for legitimate suffering." Real quickly, let's observe the definition of neurosis so everyone understands what is being talked about here. Neurosis is a mental and emotional disorder that affects only part of the personality; it is accompanied by a less distorted perception of reality than in psychosis and is accompanied by various physical, physiological, and mental disturbances (such as depression, anxieties, or phobias) Another definition given was a mental condition that is not caused by organic disease, involving symptoms of stress (depression, anxiety, obsessive behavior, hypochondria) but not a radical loss of touch with reality. The author goes on to explain how humans try to avoid suffering so much to the extent that we cause ourselves this mental illness/disorder. Why would we do that? That's a great question. He answers this question by suggesting that we tend to avoid the problems life throws at us due to fearing the pain, frustration, grief, sadness, loneliness, guilt, regret, anger, fear, anxiety, anguish, or despair that facing these problems will bring us. We either hope them to go away, ignore them, try to forget them, or pretend they do not exist. In other words, we attempt to get out of them instead of suffering through them. He goes on to suggest that this tendency to avoid problems and the emotional suffering we may find in them is the primary basis of all human mental illnesses. How many of you reading this can HONESTLY look back over your life and see or admit that you have been guilty of this? Every one of us reading should be raising our hand or shaking our head in agreement because the reality is that no one wants to suffer any of the above-listed emotions that problems bring. However, we must understand that we will ALWAYS have problems in this life. Absolutely no one is exempt from them. I wonder what could happen if we could perceive our problems for what they really are, a distinguishing between success and failure, a calling forth of our courage and our wisdom, or an opportunity to grow mentally and spiritually. It is in the process of meeting and solving problems that life has its meaning. We learn and grow through the pain of confronting and resolving problems.

The writer continues to share that going to extraordinary lengths to avoid our problems and the suffering they cause and trying to find an easy way out will bring the substitute of Neurosis, as mentioned previously. The substitute itself becomes MORE painful and MORE of a problem than the legitimate suffering of the problem it was designed to avoid! It now becomes your biggest problem! Wow, what an insight! I invite those of you reading this to pause for a moment and fully grasp this concept, and wholeheartedly declare, "NO MORE!" No more will I avoid the problems of life and the suffering that may occur because, in doing so, I am stunting my growth. Listen friends, problems demand growth from us. If you stop growing, you become stuck. If you are stuck for too long, your spirit will begin to shrivel. Decide with me today that you will welcome the problems and the pain of problems so that you can solve them and, in turn, achieve mental and spiritual health and therefore pass it down to younger generations! That is a purpose in itself! Remember, your success and growth is not just for you; It's also for your children, and their children, and generations after you!

If you are on board to now welcome the problems of life and face them head-on, let me provide you with four techniques or tools of discipline that the author encourages to experience the pain of problem-solving constructively.

The first is delaying of gratification. Delaying gratification is a process of scheduling the pain and pleasure of life in such a way as to enhance the pleasure by meeting and experiencing the pain first and getting it over with. The author gives an example of this by suggesting that in your eight-hour workday, try to accomplish the unpleasant part of your job first and end it with the more enjoyable parts of the job. Basically, save the best for last. So, in certain life problems, we could see it as getting the pain or suffering of your problem over with first so that it's out of the way, and now you can enjoy the life before you.

The Second is acceptance of responsibility. We must accept responsibility of a problem before we can solve it. You cannot solve a problem by saying, "It's not my problem" or hoping someone else will solve it for you. You must be able to say, "This is my problem, and it's up to me to solve it."

The third is dedication to the truth. Truth is reality; that which is false is unreal. Most people choose to ignore this because our route to reality is not easy. The more clearly we see the reality of the world, the better equipped we are to deal with the world. The less clearly we see the world, the more our minds are confused by falsehood, misperceptions, and illusions, and the less able we will be to determine correct courses of action and make wise decisions. Truth or reality is avoided when it is painful. We can revise our view of reality when we have the discipline to overcome that pain. To have this discipline, we must be totally dedicated to the truth.

The fourth is balancing. Balancing is the discipline required to discipline, discipline. Balancing is the discipline that gives us flexibility. For example, a flexible response system is needed to be able to handle our anger with full adequacy and competence. To know how to deal with our anger in different ways and in different situations, matching the right time with the right style of expression. Balancing is a discipline because the act of giving something up is painful. However, if you want to go far in life, it's important to give up things that don't contribute to your growth. This may include letting go of spontaneous anger, as well as any personality traits, behavior patterns, or ideologies that hold you back from growth. These are major forms of giving up that are required if one is to make significant progress in life.

In conclusion, this chapter has shed light on the importance of embracing problems and facing them head-on rather than avoiding them. The author encourages the use of these four techniques or tools of discipline to experience the pain of problem-solving constructively. By embracing these techniques, we can develop the discipline and mindset necessary to overcome challenges and make significant progress in our lives. I can truly say that if I had known the insights and tools mentioned above while going through my own time of despondency, I don't think I would have remained captive for so long. This is why I bring this to you. I want you to have every possible tool to help you achieve positive mental health! Your mind is the most valuable asset you possess. It is the key to unlocking your potential and achieving your dreams. Your mind has the power to shape your reality and to create the life that you want to live. So, I encourage you to work diligently to protect it and provide it with all the necessary nourishment so that you can reach your fullest potential in life.

Reflective Questions

1. What are some problems that you personally may have been avoiding that you can confront? How has this avoidance affected your mental well-being?

2. Have you recognized the importance of embracing problems as opportunities for growth and learning? How can you shift your perspective to see problems as a means to develop courage, wisdom, and resilience?

3. Are you willing to practice the four techniques of discipline mentioned (delaying gratification, accepting responsibility, dedication to the truth, and balancing)? How can you implement these disciplines in your life to constructively experience the pain of problem-solving and achieve mental and spiritual health?

PRAYER

Dear Heavenly Father,
Thank you for the insights gained from this chapter. Help me to embrace my problems instead of avoiding them so that I do not stunt my growth. Grant me the strength to face suffering and grow through it. Guide me in delaying gratification, accepting responsibility, seeking truth, and finding balance, so that I can constructively experience the pain of problem-solving. Give me the discernment to know what things I need to give up that do not contribute to my growth. Protect my mind and help me unlock my fullest potential.
In Jesus Name, Amen.

CHAPTER 7 CHAPTER

THE VICTORY

After receiving the life-changing word from God that my purpose had not plateaued, I embarked on my journey to hope, peace, and purpose. Along this transformative path, God orchestrated a divine connection leading me to a very special person. I thought I was connecting with this special individual for a job opportunity. However, little did I know that God had a completely different purpose for our connection. Through this individual, I was connected to a group of people who strived for mental and financial greatness. It wasn't until I got into live sessions with these people that God showed me how far off and out of sync my mental state was from his will. Every day, I attended their live sessions that discussed the importance of maintaining a positive mental state and achieving greatness. I felt both inspired and convicted as I longed for the type of positive mindset that they had. Soon after, I realized God had placed me in this space to work on my mind, as it was a major obstacle holding me back from many aspects of life, including pursuing my purpose! Upon realization of this, I began the journey to change my mindset.

Over the course of a year, this special person that came into my life challenged me to reevaluate my thoughts and mindset. She pushed me to create a positive mental state and trash the old negative one and gave me direction on how to reach my fullest potential through a mental transformation! My deliverance from hopelessness didn't come all at once. It also didn't come by one particular sermon preached or by one specific prayer prayed. It came by first a realization of what needed to change, then a hunger/desire for better and more, next I had to activate hope to attain the things I desired, and lastly, believe and have faith that there was something more and better for me and I was going to receive it! But it didn't stop there, friends, because remember, faith requires action. Faith without works is dead, right? So, I had to put my faith into action by changing the way I thought and talked, which meant thinking and speaking positively about myself and my life and refusing to allow myself to entertain any negativity. Was it easy? Absolutely not. I had to be proactive. I found an affirmation app on my phone that allowed me to set reminders to affirm myself, my faith, and my thoughts. I made time in my busy schedule to listen to something that would positively feed my soul and my faith. I posted reminders of the words God spoke over my life so that I would be constantly reminded, and so my faith would not fail. I had to remind myself to speak the promises of God and to remember his faithfulness when hard situations arose and I didn't see the things I desired in front of me. I had to cultivate a prayer life that would keep me connected to God. I had to make an effort to stay in the word of God every day. Even breaking free and being delivered from the crippling anxiety that I faced required taking action on my part. I listened to messages that gave me an understanding of anxiety. Also, one day during an altar call at church, the minister specifically called for those dealing with anxiety, and I had to swallow my pride and walk up there. This day I asked God to deliver me from it completely, and I humbly surrendered it at the feet of Jesus, firmly believing that my prayer had been answered. One of the messages I had previously listened to mentioned how the enemy will try to come against you after you have been delivered. Sure enough, that night, I had an anxiety attack for absolutely no reason. I became angry and took authority over this situation; I claimed my deliverance and resisted the enemy and his tactics, as the Bible teaches. I then put my words into action and started to praise and worship God and thank him for his peace that was now mine. Needless to say, it worked, and I was able to go back to sleep in peace. When I woke up the next day, I remember feeling incredibly light, almost as if I were floating as I walked. That day I knew I had been set free. Friends, as previously stated, you can hope and believe all day long and still stay in the exact same place. To move from where you are into greater requires true faith, and true faith will always require ACTION.

During my time of despair and introspection regarding my life's purpose, I remember conversing with God and questioning why he would give me the talent/gift of writing if I was never going to use it. I asked why he would pour into me if I had no avenue to pour out to others. I even asked him to stop giving me so much material and inspiration as it was just sitting in a notebook on a bookshelf collecting dust. Here I was, thinking God was the one holding me back from using my gifts and talents by not providing me with the opportunities to use them or the finances needed. As if I should be able to simply sit back and wait for everything to effortlessly fall into place. When in reality, it was my responsibility to get up and take action and rise above complacency. It was my job to seek after it and to find the open doors that God had already provided. It was up to me to get in the rooms and have conversations with people who could offer the opportunities. This experience taught me a timely lesson: if you desire to use your talents and gifts, especially to fulfill your purpose in life, you must be ready and willing to take action. I can't help but think of the parable Jesus shared of the three individuals who were given talents and how I now realize it was really a call to action. They had to decide whether to multiply what they had been given or let it go to waste. Would they put forth work and thought to find a way for it to increase? We can recall in the parable how the man who was given one buried it. Maybe he thought, "If I had more, then I definitely could do something with it, but this ONE is just not enough." Maybe he feared that he would fail if he tried to increase it. Perhaps that negative thought rooted in fear caused him to sit on it and not even try. Maybe he was like me and questioned the one who gave it. "Why would you give me this but not give me any instruction on what to do with it?" "Why don't you tell me exactly where to go and exactly what to do to make the most of it?" Because, in all honesty, don't we all want the reassurance and ease of knowing exactly what to do, say, and where to go to reach the fullest potential and success of what we have been given? I feel we can gather from this story that; Jesus doesn't necessarily give it to us the easy way. I'm realizing that the true lesson is an overall message of taking action. Yes, he is always there to provide and make ways, but I solely believe he wants to see us putting our best efforts and commitment into what we have been given.

As I began this new journey of taking action through faith, God stepped in and started blessing and showing his faithfulness. In prayer, I began to declare in full faith things that I did not currently see before me but believed they could be my reality. I not only declared them, I asked God for a divine strategy to reach them. In no time at all, God began honoring my hope, faith, and actions. Those things I declared and began acting on started coming to pass. In the spirit of transparency to encourage your faith, one testimony that comes to mind is when my husband and I specifically prayed and claimed an increase in our credit scores. This is one thing we declared would be done by the end of that current year. We knew we would need some extra money to reach that goal. Unfortunately, we had no extra money to put towards this. Through prayer and seeking different options to help us in this area, God started providing my husband with these unique little jobs that allowed him to earn extra income without sacrificing time with our family. For the next couple of months, these opportunities came in abundance. We were able to pay off debt and hire someone to help us get the credit reports cleaned up, and within a few more months, our credit scores increased significantly! Around the same time, my husband began searching for a better job. We applied the principle of sowing and reaping and sowed into the release of a new job in faith. We hoped, had faith, and he took action by applying to jobs and going on interviews. We waited patiently, fully persuaded that God would honor our faith and the right job would come. Within no time, God came through and gave the increase. My husband was offered a new job that provided a significant increase in all areas! I could go on and list many more testimonies from this time. However, this journey has taught us the power of hope, faith, and taking action in alignment with God's plan as He faithfully fulfills His promises.

After putting in hard work to upgrade my mental health, I began to see the hand of God work in my life like never before. For example, during this time of my life, I had never gotten to work in my gift of writing. As briefly mentioned above, I was always writing. Whether in my journal, songs, or poems. Writing was an escape and an outlet I often used to help me process things happening in life. I always said I could write better than I could speak. Doing something within my gift of writing was a dream I had forgotten all about due to the state of hopelessness I got tangled up in. As I was on this positive mental journey, one thing led to another, and I had the opportunity to not only attend a course for writing screenplays, but after completion of the course, God opened a door for me to be able to write a pilot for an upcoming Christian television series with a continued writing gig for the remainder of the episodes. Not only did I get to write, but I also got a position as co-director as they loved my vision/creativity for the show. This didn't happen effortlessly. It took me getting into the right conversations with the right people and asserting myself. It took finding the open doors and walking through them. This was something I had NEVER even dreamed I would do; it literally was never on my bucket list, as I never had the capacity to dream or imagine I would be able to do something like this. It was easily one of the best moments of my life and awakened me to a newfound belief that I can truly do anything with God on my side when I ignite my hope and faith and combine them with action! The Lord continued to open doors, leading me and my husband to an incredible opportunity as co-owners of PsalmStream, Inc., a production company committed to delivering captivating family media content. This venture not only aligns with our passion but also provides us with the means to allow us to pursue many other creative endeavors that we have long desired. Fast forward to now, never in a million years did I ever think I would be writing a book encouraging others to come out of what I myself was bound in, but here I am. All those journals collecting dust ended up being the very content I would use for this book! I am proof that God really does do EXCEEDING, ABUNDANTLY, ABOVE what you could ask or think! So, to every mother or father out there, you have dedicated so much of your time and energy to your family, and that in itself is a great accomplishment. It will always be your purpose to parent your children, be there for them, and teach them about the love of God and who he is. But it's important to remember that you are more than just a mother or a father. You have unique skills, talents, and passions waiting to be discovered and pursued. This also goes for anyone reading this book who may not be a parent. You are more than just a wife or husband or just an employee. Remember, you are strong, capable, and deserving of a happy and fulfilling life. Keep pushing forward, and don't give up on yourself. The world needs your unique gifts and talents, and I can't wait to see all that you will accomplish. I implore you to believe with me today that there is more to your story, and your purpose has not plateaued!

THE END

Biblical Affirmations

I am fearfully and wonderfully made in the image of God. (Psalm 139:14)

I am forgiven of all my sins through the grace of Jesus Christ. (Ephesians 1:7)

I am a child of God, and He loves me unconditionally. (1 John 3:1)

I am chosen and called by God for a purpose. (1 Peter 2:9)

I am more than a conqueror through Christ who strengthens me. (Romans 8:37)

I am the righteousness of God in Christ Jesus. (2 Corinthians 5:21)

I am blessed and highly favored by God. (Ephesians 1:3)

I am a new creation in Christ, old things have passed away. (2 Corinthians 5:17)

I am filled with the Holy Spirit, who guides and empowers me. (Acts 1:8)

I am a temple of the Holy Spirit, and God's Spirit dwells in me. (1 Corinthians 6:19)

I am healed by the stripes of Jesus. (1 Peter 2:24)

I am beloved by God more fully than I could ever imagine. (Ephesians 3:18)

I am an overcomer through faith in Jesus Christ. (1 John 5:4)

I am a vessel of God's love, and I can share His love with others. (1 John 4:7)

I am filled with joy and peace that surpasses all understanding. (Romans 15:13)

I am a light in the world, shining the love and truth of God. (Matthew 5:14)

I am blessed with spiritual blessings in heavenly places. (Ephesians 1:3)

I am equipped with the armor of God to stand against the enemy. (Ephesians 6:11)

I am called to walk in humility and serve others with love. (Galatians 5:13)

I am an ambassador for Christ, spreading the good news of salvation. (2 Corinthians 5:20)

I can do all things through Christ who strengthens me. (Philippians 4:13)

I can trust in the Lord with all my heart and lean not on my own understanding. (Proverbs 3:5)

I can be strong and courageous, for the Lord is with me wherever I go. (Joshua 1:9)

I can seek first the kingdom of God and His righteousness, and all things will be added unto me. (Matthew 6:33)

I can be still and know that He is God. (Psalm 46:10)

I can cast all my anxieties on Him because He cares for me.

(1 Peter 5:7)

I can take delight in the Lord, and He will give me the desires of my heart. (Psalm 37:4)

I can be confident that He who began a good work in me will carry it on to completion. (Philippians 1:6)

I can love my enemies and pray for those who persecute me. (Matthew 5:44)

I can walk in wisdom and make the most of every opportunity. (Colossians 4:5)

Non-Biblical Affirmations

I am capable of overcoming any challenge that comes my way.

I am deserving of love, happiness, and success.

I am constantly growing and evolving into the best version of myself.

I am surrounded by a supportive and positive community.

I am resilient and can bounce back from setbacks with strength.

I am in control of my own happiness and choose to focus on the positive.

I am talented and have unique gifts to share with the world.

I am worthy of self-care and prioritize my well-being.

I am open to new opportunities and embrace change with enthusiasm.

I am confident in my abilities and trust my intuition.

I am a magnet for abundance and attract prosperity into my life.

I am grateful for all the blessings in my life and find joy in the present moment.

I am surrounded by beauty and find inspiration in the world around me.

I am patient and trust that everything unfolds in divine timing.

I am courageous and step outside my comfort zone to achieve my dreams.

I am a problem solver and find creative solutions to any obstacles.

I am worthy of success and embrace the journey of growth.

I am blessed with a positive mindset that empowers me in all aspects of life.

I am kind and compassionate, spreading love and kindness wherever I go.

I am enough just as I am, and I embrace my unique qualities and strengths.

I am a confident and capable individual, capable of achieving my goals.

I am in control of my thoughts and emotions, and I choose to cultivate positivity.

I am surrounded by love and support, and I attract positive relationships into my life.

I am worthy of abundance and prosperity, and I welcome it into my life.

I am constantly evolving and growing, embracing personal development and self-improvement.

I am deserving of success, and I am confident in my ability to achieve it.

I am open to receiving and giving unconditional love in all areas of my life.

I am living a life filled with purpose and passion, making a positive impact on the world.

I am grateful for the abundance that flows into my life in various forms.

I am resilient, and I embrace challenges as opportunities for growth and transformation.

HOW TO REACH ME

Email: info@yourpurposehasnotplateaued.com

Website: www.YourPurposeHasNotPlateaued.com

Facebook: Kaitlin Miller

ABOUT THE AUTHOR

Meet Kaitlin, a devoted mother of two boys and a loving wife who has always had a passion for writing. From the young age of seven, she discovered her love for storytelling, crafting songs, poems, and short stories. Her creative pursuits led her to write a pilot episode for a television series. She also took on the role of co-director for this project. Together with her husband, Kaitlin is part of PsalmStream Inc., a company dedicated to releasing engaging family media content. They are excited about the future and the impact they can make. Through her work, she aims to create content that brings joy and valuable life lessons to audiences of all ages.